## *About The Aut,*

When I found out I had ALS at the age of 29, I began to see what is really important. Waiting for what I truly wanted to experience began to seem silly with the potential shortening of my life at hand. But I didn't think of ALS as a death sentence then and I don't now, a year later. In fact, while I search for ways to heal I have come to see it as an opportunity in many ways, to grow into an expanded sense of love, joy, gratitude, and peace; those things I always yearned for yet found myself too busy to give proper time to. In this ALS is the great simplifier, reducing physical function so that the only choice given is to look within as outer responsibilities fall away. And as I look, love is what I'm finding. Both self-love so long withheld and compassion for all people in the recognition that we are all in this together, this crazy ride called life. We each have our burdens to bear, and while no one can carry them for us we can offer one another the love that is our true nature, making life a little bit lighter for one another, and in so doing make the world a better place.

It is from this perspective that I wrote the poems in this book, most of which have little to do with ALS itself but carry the seeds of learning I am gathering on this journey. I hope that the words in this book find you in whatever way they are meant to and that in some way they lift you up. In love and gratitude, Ryan.

# Seeds of
# Light Sown

# Seeds of
# Light Sown

*Soulful Poems By:*

Ryan Farnsworth

## Special Thanks To:

Asher Garfinkel, Jenica Lancy, and Daniel Potapshyn at
the ALS Association Golden West Chapter for your
friendship and the incredible work you do in raising
funds and awareness for ALS research and care for
people living with ALS like myself, and for sharing my
poetry within the community. Julie Sands Donaldson at
Metabolic Healing for your friendship and generosity
in sharing your time and knowledge for my continued
wellbeing, and for writing this book's beautiful
foreword. Sandy Stillwell for giving me a copy of: "In a
Dress Made of Butterflies," which has helped to inspire
me in seeing what a well-formatted and beautiful book
of poems looks like.

## Copyright and Contact Info:

Ryan Farnsworth
P.O. Box 241
Yountville, CA, 94599

Email: groundrising@gmail.com
Facebook: www.facebook.com/ryan.farnsworth.52

This book is dedicated to the friends and family that have made my life lighter by showering me with love and support during these trying times. In particular my mom, whose love and nurturing energy has helped me to remain strong and keep my gaze skyward, and to my dad whose steadfast support and friendship has helped me to keep an even keel.

# Contents:

## Growth of Seed and Soul

## Songs of Love and the Sound of Silence

## From Dreams and Depth of Sea

## The Mind and Moments of Presence

## *Foreword:*

I have learned in this life that when it becomes difficult to describe someone or something with words, I am in the presence of true grace. This is my experience with Ryan Farnsworth.

I became acquainted with Ryan through a professional relationship. Some of his first words to me were "I've taken it upon myself to heal myself to the best of my ability." To the best of Ryan's ability is a measure quite large for most of us...he approaches both healing and life like a calm and confident champion, deeply rooted in his body and mind.

I am inspired by this book Ryan is putting forth, and inspired by all he knows about the beauty of life and the grace of challenge.

In Ryan's case, ALS stands for Acclaimed Laureate Sensor! Congratulations and Godspeed to you, my dear friend, and to all those you dream to touch.

*Julie Sands Donaldson, CMTA & LMT*
*VP & Dir. of Client & Clinical Services at Metabolic Healing*

# Seeds of
# Light Sown

# Growth of
## Seed and Soul

Rising up through the cracks,
Of challenges faced we grow,
Reaching toward the light,
In remembering the truth,
Of who we really are.

## Gardeners of Intention

We are planting every second,
These thoughts as seeds sown,
To be grown within the soil,
Of the subconscious mind.

This ground within us grows,
Whatever thoughts we give it,
Nurturing seeds of love and joy,
Or weeds without preference.

For we choose what we wish to plant,
While the soil within us can only agree,
Accepting these grains of future,
And forming them into reality.

In an elegantly beautiful simplicity,
What we plant is what comes to be,
And becomes the steps we take,
The choices we make.

Those thoughts we think most often,
We are watering in repetition's rain,
And the light of our attention shines,
On what our ideal world contains.

We must master mindful gardening,
For weeds with little water grow,
While love and joy need practice,
And careful cultivation.

So let us sow seeds of intention,
In knowing what we wish to grow,
By watering whatever we wish to be,
Within this ever-growing reality.

## *Watering the Seed Within*

Seeking,
Safety within,
Heart's heavy shield,
A soul seed,
Sleeps.

Buried,
Behind walls,
Blocking love sought,
With safety,
Bought.

Longing,
For words said,
Times too few,
To come,
True:

"I love myself,
I love who I am,
I love you."

With words,
Lovingly spoken,
Walls break open,
Casting bricks,
Aside.

In love's,
Light showered,
Finally feeling safe,
The soul seed,
Opens.

## Gods of Growth

The wind begins to bluster,
Mustering into a tempest,
Tame skies transformed,
As surging clouds gather,
The God of Storm.

Lightning slashes through sky,
Dark clouds cracking open,
Spilling water into wind,
Drops wildly dancing,
While they descend.

A pitter-pattering of drops,
Becomes a showering symphony,
As a million falling spheres magnify,
Mother earth drinking deeply,
From the sky.

Dirt dampens as water seeps,
Into soil where seeds sleep,
Yawning open in the ground,
While waking from dry dreams,
Happily drowned.

Faster time begins to flow,
Growing like the green shoots,
Rising through the damp dark,
Weaving ever-upward,
Seeking light's spark.

Sprouting out from soil beds,
Buried seedlings burst forth,
Bringing end to their night,
The brightly shining sun,
God of Light.

## In Earth's Soil Planted (For Aunt Cookie)

As God's light contained within a seed,
We shoot forth from the starry heavens,
Some bright source since forgotten,
And finding mother's fertile womb,
We begin to grow in loving soil.

In time transplanted from womb to world,
We remain rooted in the remembrance,
Of the infinite love from which we came,
As naked souls with unfettered hearts,
Unhardened by worry or hardship.

But growing up we shoot roots down,
Deeper into this planet's rocky soil,
Finding on Earth it is tough to thrive,
With bills and responsibilities rising,
We want more than to just survive.

We long for a deeper lasting connection,
Counting on family for steady foundation,
Helping to carry us through hardships,
As we rise together toward the sun,
Flowering in shared light.

Love is the water with which we grow,
And we begin to see and know life anew,
From gratitude and love rather than lack,
Living for the many precious moments,
That compose this beautiful life.

So when we see that the years grow long,
And dusk is dawning upon our days,
We can look back at a life well-lived,
Surrounded by family and friends,
While enveloped in love.

And then reaching to God we return,
Carrying with us the lessons learned,
And in life's growth gained now we soar,
For though the body's light has faded,
The soul shines brighter than ever before.

# Songs of Love
# & the Sound
# Of Silence

Pure and bright,
Moments of love,
Sing without words,
In language we all understand.

## The Sound of the Soul

The music of the soul stirs within,
A subtle sound to the untrained ear,
Accustomed to the chaos and clamor of the world.

Within we hear the melody rising,
Sounding sweetly of simple joy,
Of happiness for its own sake,
Like the brightly smiling child,
You once knew to be yourself.

# *Music of Life*

Enveloped in a still and present peace,
Made possible by meditation's magic,
I listen to the music of the world,
Playing outside my window.

Here the breeze conducts a chorus,
Of windblown whispering leaves,
Sighing and singing soothingly,
As their song my ears perceive.

A fountain flows in ceaseless conversation,
Like the unbroken language of a brook,
Never lacking in words to describe,
Its dancing sense of flow imbibed.

The finches too find their songs,
In shrill conversational cadence,
While seeking seed in the feeder,
Chirping out their musical conveyance.

These sounds each are notes of song,
But silence too plays it part in music,
And the calm stillness within me mirrors,
The deep quiet behind the sounds.

So silence and sound weave together,
As rising and falling melodies played,
While I listen outside my window,
To the world's beautiful music made.

## A Worldwide Awakening

In dreams of discord we unsoundly slept,
A silence drawn long across these years,
While like sleeping songbirds we waited,
For the spark of light's dawn to draw near.

We tossed, turned, and yearned in waiting,
For a bright star to pierce the veil of night,
That like a dark shroud had obscured,
The awareness of our own inner light.

But finally that fiery spark of potential,
Is piercing the deep fabric of dream,
As the earth is washed in sun-cast light,
And we are awakening it seems.

There is a stirring within the silence,
And a sense of suspense within the air,
Until a delicate song shatters the quiet,
In a voice joyous like a grateful prayer.

How sweetly that sound lifts skyward,
Rising as its notes of celebration ring,
Rippling out across the awakening world,
Inspiring others to stand and sing.

Millions now join together in jubilant song,
As more souls cast sleep's silence aside,
Harmonizing in this heartfelt melody,
Washing the world in its tide.

Within this collective chorus of awakening,
The whole world sings under the risen sun,
As the silence and darkness are fleeing,
And a new time on earth has begun.

## Love like Water

Love is an important part of who and what I am,
But in my wayward distraction within the world,
I neglected to water my heart with its attention.

Loving other people has always come naturally to me,
But something important was missing on my path,
And I had forgotten how to love myself.

But gradually in remembrance I began to grow,
Being guided by a stirring in my heart and soul,
Like a thirst for the love that I lacked.

My heart was dry in this lasting drought of love,
But now I pour love like water on myself,
And my parched heart gratefully drinks it in.

I still forget to shower myself in this love sometimes,
But in remembering I find realignment with life's flow,
And in love's pure water all that is good within me grows.

## Driving with Family

The sun lazily slides toward the hills of the Napa Valley,
As amber light filters through the leaves of passing trees,
Like beams of warm honey that  slow this moment in time.

We are talking and laughing together as a family,
And I find myself filled with the simple yet powerful joy,
That finds me when my heart is open and my mind is still.

# From Dreams
## & Depths
### Of Sea

Slipping into sleep we emerge from the sea,
Riding moonbeams into that blissful infinity,
Unrestrained but lovingly held;
Free.

## Like Light Remembered

How many lives I have lived I cannot say,
But there is such perfection in this design,
Of daring to forget my past lives in this lifetime,
For the sake of focusing on a singular path,
Undistracted by previous roads travelled.

I cannot claim to understand how it works,
Yet I envision it like being born into the ocean,
Leaving my past lives like the light behind me,
On the surface now far above and forgotten,
While I experience life in the depths of sea.

Even with the surface unknown to me I ascend,
Guided to swim upward from the dark depths,
Holding tightly to a vague memory of light,
Like a vivid dream that seems so real,
I have come to trust it is true.

And as if rewarded for following my faith,
Strands of light begin to pierce the darkness,
As I rise from depths toward the shimmering surface,
Finding flickering remembrances along the way,
Of the light that is guiding me home.

## Emergence

Far beneath the surface shimmering above,
With lungs taut trying to breathe what little is left,
I propel myself upward defiant against death.

Rising, Rising! The air so close...
As the surface finally breaks,
In an explosion of light and breath!

## Sinking Below the Surface

Thoughts like the tide come and go,
A flow that rarely falters or fades,
In ceaseless swaying on the surface,
Like rolling waves on the sea.

Through our days we are often drifting,
Upon this rhythmic swell of thought,
Lulling us within its ocean's wake,
In a daydream we so rarely break.

Sometimes it is subtle enough to forget,
Or at times it can be like the sea in storm,
With waves crashing in a tempest of thought,
And we within that turmoil are caught.

But in meditation we can learn dive below,
Even in the midst of mental squall or storm,
Where a calmness exists under the sea,
In an undisturbed tranquility.

It takes patience to sink into presence,
Letting the churning waves slowly settle,
When so choppy are the mind's motions,
To find peace and quiet within the ocean.

Here serenity abides beneath the surface,
Offering peace from the turbulent tides,
To find a calm where all remains still,
When we can learn to dive at will.

## The Great Oak Tree

On a hill beneath the boughs of a massive oak I sit,
With its bark at my back and having nowhere to be,
But under its shade while the sun burns above,
And sleep eventually takes me…

In dream I am facing The Great Oak Tree,
Which stands in strength and wisdom,
Beckoning me to place my palm,
Against its ancient bark.

I do, and the world begins to sway,
As lines and definitions fall away,
And suddenly I am no longer 'me,'
But The Great Oak Tree,
I Am.

I find I am gnarled wood and bark embodied,
　　　Towering trunk, limb, and branch.
I am a network of roots reaching deep into soil,
　　　Seeking water's wetness.
I am with laden with leaf beyond counting,
　　　My collectors of sun-cast light.
I am The Great Oak Tree to Earth anchored,
　　　And this ground is my home.

At night the sky is my ceaseless ceiling,
As I marvel up at the endless expanse of space,
In which a billion bright stars splay out above,
Scattered across an unfathomable infinity,
As blinking expressions of divine love.

It is in an ever-unfolding moment that I live,
Measuring time not in ticking seconds,
But by the sun's conducting of light and dark,
Or the moon's spanning of starry skies,

In these time's passing I mark.

I exalt in the simple joy and beauty of being,
Gathering yearly rings of growth around me,
Like the light and liquid life on which I thrive,
And as the present moment pushes forward,
Each day is a new reason to be alive.

Through the ceaseless shifting of seasons,
From tiny acorn to sapling to towering tree,
Life playfully dances and sings around me,
And from this rooted perspective I perceive,
What it truly means to Be.

Then drawn from the dream I return,
Finding bark once again at my back,
Though the sun had somewhat strayed,
Nearer to the hillside while I slept,
Under the Great Oak's shade.

I realize I can walk from this spot,
And travel to whatever place I please,
But the urge to stay is somehow stronger,
For in rooted remembrance I remain,
And decide to sit a while longer.

# The Mind
# & Moments
# Of Presence

I find my mind moving most,
When I wish it to be still,
To keep me ever-thinking,
It does what it will.

## When We Slow Enough to See

We search for fulfillment in these facets of life,
Expanding outward to find what we seek.

It shimmers within the rippling waters of reality,
A half-formed remembrance waiting to be found.

It is the treasure we seek during many miles of walking,
Only to be found when the mind finally stops,
       And the water stills.

## Truth Remembered

The whole of existence happens,
Within a single ever-present moment,
That can be experienced but never known.

All that has ever occurred happened in a time called Now,
All that will ever occur will happen in a time called Now,
This gift of life given to us can only be experienced Now.

## The Mind's Moon

Rotating slow and lazy circles in space,
The contented Earth warms herself,
Under the bright fire-cast light,
From the distantly dawning,
Ever-smiling Sun.

The Moon jealously watches,
Waning in reflected false-light,
Rotating circles around reality,
Yet seeing itself as the center,
Of all creation.

Truth it so distantly touches,
With an objective perspective,
A cold logic lacking love's warmth,
Like a mind missing the point of life,
Waiting for it to live itself.

This is the problem when we see,
Life through lacking lenses,
Like a thing incomplete,
We venture out too far,
Toward other stars...

When here and now is what we seek.

## Flickering Frames

Now,
A single moment,
Birthed into being,
Between future and past,
Replaced in a blink,
With a new,
Now.

Now,
Frames of life,
Flicker and flash,
In a seamless flow,
Ever-present,
Ever-new,
Now.

Now,
Where we breathe,
Where we live and be,
When we choose,
When we see,
Now.

## Mental Fishing

In meditation I am like a fish,
While my mind like a fisherman,
Casts thoughts like lures before me,
To see with what I will agree.

I sit stock-still with back erect,
Letting my swimming thoughts slow,
While all manner of alluring bait,
Cross my awareness while I wait.

"What new meal is this?" I wonder,
While the bait meanders my way,
In silver shimmering splendor,
"It must be my lucky day!"

So taken am I with the thought,
That I forget about stillness sought,
And in seeing the lure's seductive light,
I can do nothing else but bite!

Then caught by the line of thought,
My meditation quickly melts away,
Along with the present moment,
While my mind pulls me astray.

But in the end I always return,
To this present moment in time,
When my mind is done wandering,
And to peace and stillness I realign.

## Old Wisdom Gained Young

I have never heard the elderly lament,
In wishing that they would have lived less,
Having packed too much life into their years.

I imagine instead that as their tired suns sink,
Back towards the horizon of their lives,
Each moment becomes more precious.

If asked for advice such an old one might say:

> Don't put your dreams on a shelf labeled 'someday',
> A day in the future when there will be more time,
> For time waits for no one.

> Live the life you want and do not wait or hesitate,
> While you are healthy and have the physical function,
> To spend your time in all of the ways you prefer.

And I think to myself:
We should not need to grow old,
To gain such wisdom.

## Returning

Places and things I have seen that may never come to be,
And I've sought solace within bright shards of memory,
Finding myself stretched thin across 'if', 'when', and 'then',
Now I return to you.

Finding you at first only in those fleeting moments,
Weak and weary from some long journey nowhere,
You wait for me where you have always been,
Now I return to you.

In your presence I find more of myself,
As I awaken to this gift of life I am living,
Always new and bright and beautiful,
Now I return to you…

And I am so very grateful to be here.

# Poems of Prayer & Hope Held

My edges soften as time flows faster,
And even the air begins to vibrate,
With the promise of things to come.

## ALS Prayer

God I now affirm this return to wellness,
That has begun and is already done,
For within your timeless presence,
All things that come into existence,
Occur within the infinite space of Now.

I am open to your bright and healing light,
That is shining like a gem within my heart,
Singing as a glorious hymn to your love,
For I have come to recognize,
That that is what I am.

May my mind and heart be unburdened,
Of all fears, worries, and thoughts of lack,
In bringing me back into balance with you,
For I feel that there is so much more,
That I am here to do.

## *Healing Prayer*

Let every cell within me rejoice,
In the gift that this moment brings,
Alive in precious song that sings,
As healing weaves within me.

Like music played from memory,
This loving light knows what I need,
As imbalances within me recede,
In the wake of wellness restored.

## Gratitude Prayer

God I wish to thank you,
For it feels that for the first time,
I am fully opening myself to receive,
The love that you are always so freely giving,
Within this beautiful process called living.

I thank you for the many miracles,
That bless my awareness each day,
Like the connection felt within a smile,
The warmth of the sun upon on my face,
Or a family member's embrace.

I thank you too for guiding my mind,
Toward words that others wish to read,
For it is my heartfelt desire to help people,
And it is my joy and passion to write,
These words that contain your light.

# A Flow of
## Words Followed

Unfolding are these lines,
Like a river's running,
Ever-forward,
I follow the flow.

## Made of Water and Wind

I dance in romance with an idea,
Fingers tapping out a flow of words,
Like water pouring from my mind,
As the words weave together,
Creative stars aligned.

It flows from me like a river runs,
But I cannot claim or catch it,
For too wild it is to be tamed,
Yet I follow where it leads,
My muse without a name.

Like grass under breeze it bends,
Weaving like wind through trees,
The river then returning to its source,
Darting deftly into the distance,
Having run its current's course.

And then I find myself alone,
That well of words run dry,
Left with a jagged and uncut gem,
Waiting to be cut and crafted,
Into something beautiful.

## Birthed to Blank Page

Letters are building blocks of meaning,
Solitary pieces of potential prose,
Brought together with purpose,
To form the words you now read.

Like letters words hate to be alone,
Wishing to written in such a way,
As to be worthy of the beauty,
It is possible for them to convey.

It all starts with the mental slate,
Where we patiently wait to receive,
Or like a lightning strike conceive,
Of ideas longing for expression.

This thought or fleeting feeling,
Then translated from mind and heart,
As words poured to waiting page,
Is where the birthing starts.

In this labor of love's creation,
Ideas are then brought into form,
As a beautiful mess of words,
To page newly born.

From these lines in fragile infancy,
The idea then gradually grows,
Granted life by a spark of soul,
And by mind and heart composed.

Like strangers these lines once were,
Lacking strong connection to one another,
But as the poem nears its completion,
In stanza they are sister and brother.

And when the words feel like family,
Finally at home in these lines forged,
From heart and soul finding fusion,
The poem has reached its conclusion.

# Breaking Barriers & Layers Shed

Through the mouth of the storm comes,
Without fear or regret,
The unburdened soul.

## Unification

Pouring sunlight spills,
Like coursing liquid love,
Into my crown, mind, and heart,
And I feel a surging flow,
As the opening starts.

A dawning brightness swells,
Like a wave of surging love,
Melting locks that lack keys,
While crashing down doors,
Hidden deep within me.

It is here that I find myself,
A small child staring back,
Trapped frozen in time,
Once forgotten,
Now found,
Free to finally Be.

## *Walls*

Those who need love the most never ask for it,
Wearing an armor of self-sufficiency,
We work hard and never ask for help,
Guarding walls hardened by time,
Secretly hoping that someone cares,
Enough to break through.

## Without Worry

When we worry about what the future holds,
We are building a bridge from 'now' to 'then',
And somehow fooling ourselves into believing,
That envisioning worst case scenarios,
Will prepare us for their possibility.

We can't act on a future that doesn't yet exist,
But we try as the present moment passes us by,
Reducing its reality to a mere stepping stone,
While worrying about what may come to pass,
In fretting on the future's imaginary contents.

It is good to be prepared for various possibilities,
But this propensity to project doubt into the future,
Merely pretends to serve a worthwhile purpose,
When in reality it is just glorified guesswork,
Energy spent on undesirable outcomes.

The mind will spin endlessly in circular motions,
While making anxious estimations and calculations,
Of a future that always finds us in an unknowable way,
And its reality will override all of our imaginings,
When that moment finally arrives.

So let us lay down this need for endless anticipation,
In which being busy becomes all we know how to be,
And place our attention instead upon the present,
Where life is unfolding in its own perfect way,
And everything will be ok without worry.

## The Prisoner and Jailor

"I am being held hostage here,
And all I want is to be free…"

*But I built this cell bar by bar,*
*And I am holding its key.*

"I am a helpless prisoner,
Kept against my will…"

*But I'm the only one here,*
*And I am paying the bill.*

"Well perhaps the time has come,
For me to open my eyes and see…"

*That the prisoner and the jailor,*
*The cell and key both are me.*

"In this newfound realization,
I can finally face these facts…"

*And as with all lessons learned,*
*What remains is to act.*

## Wisdom Watched

Wisdom herself watched,
  while I daily built my shell,

Waited while I re-learned,
  the same old lessons,

And smiled as I finally began,
  to unmake what I had made.

# Aviary
## Additions

Something within me stirs,
When broad wings spread,
Taking flight.

## The Meal

All single-minded intent and precision in design,
With wings sleek, eyes keen, and talons sharp,
The hawk's hunt begins.

The late afternoon sun beats down on the field below,
Casting a winged shadow which skirts the earth,
As the hawk spins slow circles on the breeze,
Searching...

There!
A flicker movement,
Darting quickly through the golden grass.

Hovering closer,
The hawk hangs on the wind,
Watching, waiting...

And then the dive begins,
A freefalling rush to the ground below,
Wind whistling as the earth rises up.

The distance closes quickly,
A shadow falling over the mouse,
Jumping to motion as death looms.

Talons tighten!
And find themselves empty.

## The Hummingbird I Am

Flitting amongst flowers with startling speed,
I zip around within a bright blur of swirling color,
Having forgotten in that fever of movement,
What it means to be still.

Even my pace is hurried and my hovering done in haste,
While suspended in stillness by tiny buzzing wings,
For I sip sweet honey from bright flower blossoms,
Without taking the time to savor the sweet taste.

Spring has sprung to life and the nectar flows freely,
Though my thoughts dwell on the fear of future lack,
Like strands of worry woven into webs which catch me,
Within spinning circles that seem to say:

"What if this nectar neglects to flow?"
"What if these wildflowers wither away?"

My frenzied flight continues with me caught in thought,
Fueled by the imagined future of this fearful reverie,
My mind having flown far past me into the future,
While my body flying at full speed hits a tree…

And then, nothing…
A silence seeming to stretch too far,
For far too long to return to the world,
Before being broken by the quiet flutter of a tiny heart.

I awaken, awareness like a new day dawning within me,
Rising like a bright sun burning away that fog of fear,
Worry's shroud now shed leaving clarity of sight,
While warming my soul in bright and vibrant light.

My senses gently sway within Spring's colorful symphony,
As I listen to wildflower hills humming the rhythm of life,

And a deep contented stillness settles within me,
My mind calm like a mountain lake on a windless day.

And in this silence a single thought rings out like a note,
That ripples the stillness of my consciousness like a kiss:
There is too much beauty in being alive,
To waste another moment in worry.

# A Poem

## In Closing

To those that dare to dream,
A brighter world into being,
Both within and without.

## To Those that Sow Seeds of Light

I am so honored to be on this journey with you,
Whether the miles between us be many or few,
We are walking the many paths,
Which in reality are One.

I thank you for being on Earth with me at this time,
Growing, learning, and remembering the light of love,
Which we stoke within us like a growing flame,
Burning away all of the illusions which bind us,
Shining brightly in a world that needs our light,
So that one day we may all stand unburdened and free.

We know that the change starts with and within us,
And though these paths we walk are rarely easy,
We choose the high road when we can,
Seeking out the best versions of ourselves,
While discovering the gifts we have to share.

Who we are is the true gift we are giving the world,
We, the lights making this earth a little brighter,
A little bit lighter for us having been here.

Just by being ourselves and staying true to that,
We become a blueprint for others to do the same,
So that they too may spread the seeds of love and hope,
That are now growing up through the cracks and crevices,
Flowering into the bright vision of the future,
Which we are creating as our new reality.

I am so deeply grateful and honored to be with you now,
Sharing these words that I hope have lifted your heart,
For we truly are all in this together as one family,
And each of us has a necessary part to play,
In this dawning revolution of consciousness.

## *Thanks for Reading Seeds of Light Sown!*

Thanks so much for reading Seeds of Light Sown. If you enjoyed or benefitted from these poems I would love to hear from you. Please help spread the word by writing a review of my book on Amazon, and use the information in the front pages of this book to friend request and follow me on Facebook if you wish to be notified as I release new poetry and inspirational writings.

I believe that living on Earth at this time is about love, expansion, and connection. Now faster than ever in our history we are growing on the soul level, remembering our true nature of love and seeing through illusions of separation. When the mind is quiet and the heart is open you may be able to feel the change coming like a wave, hear it singing in the whispering wind, or see it in the vibrant colors of the Earth. We truly are Seeds of Light Sown into the world, rising from a lack of light below the ground to finally burst through the soil into an expanded experience of life. That is why we are here, so let us embrace this journey as we grow together toward the light, remembering.